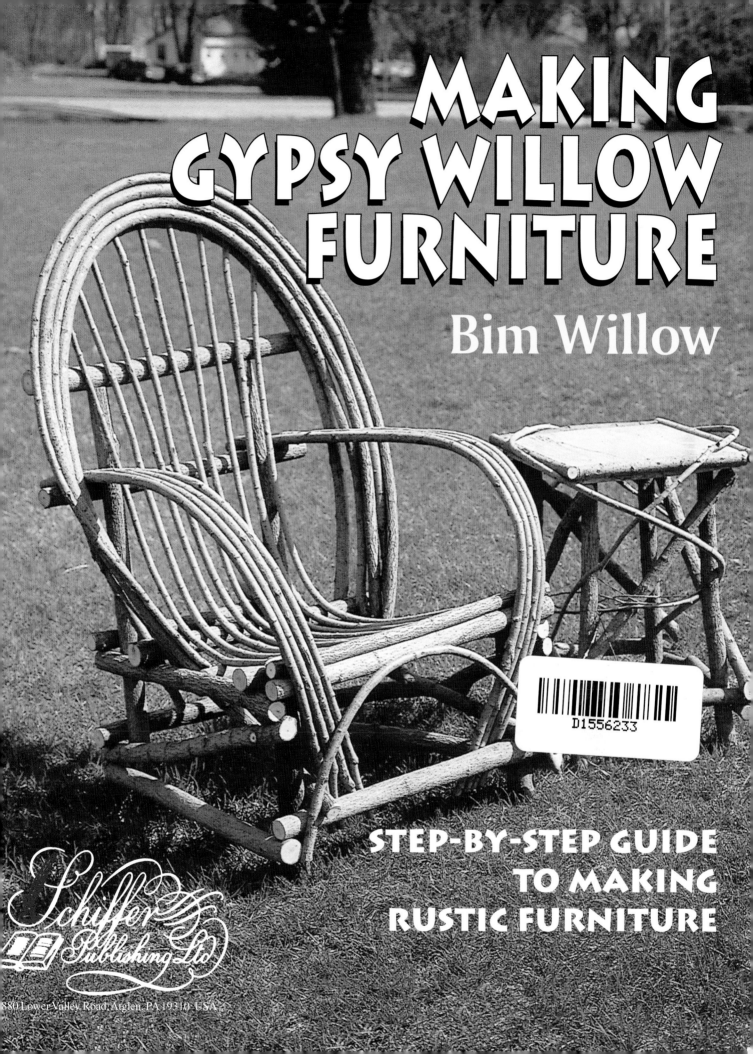

MAKING GYPSY WILLOW FURNITURE

Bim Willow

STEP-BY-STEP GUIDE TO MAKING RUSTIC FURNITURE

Schiffer Publishing Ltd
880 Lower Valley Road, Atglen, PA 19310 USA

D1556233

Library of Congress Control Number: 97-80806

This book is meant only for personal home use and recreation. It is not intended for commercial applications or manufacturing purposes.
Book designed by Laurie A. Smucker

ISBN: 978-0-7643-0407-1
Printed in China

Schiffer Books are available at special discounts for bulk purchases for sales promotions or premiums. Special editions, including personalized covers, corporate imprints, and excerpts can be created in large quantities for special needs. For more information contact the publisher:

Published by Schiffer Publishing Ltd.
4880 Lower Valley Road
Atglen, PA 19310
Phone: (610) 593-1777; Fax: (610) 593-2002
E-mail: Info@schifferbooks.com

For the largest selection of fine reference books on this and related subjects, please visit our website at
www.schifferbooks.com
We are always looking for people to write books on new and related subjects. If you have an idea for a book, please contact us at proposals@schifferbooks.com

This book may be purchased from the publisher.
Include $5.00 for shipping.
Please try your bookstore first.
You may write for a free catalog.

In Europe, Schiffer books are distributed by
Bushwood Books
6 Marksbury Ave.
Kew Gardens
Surrey TW9 4JF England
Phone: 44 (0) 20 8392 8585; Fax: 44 (0) 20 8392 9876
E-mail: info@bushwoodbooks.co.uk
Website: www.bushwoodbooks.co.uk

Introduction

As early as the age of 7 I wanted to do two things: make people laugh and create beautiful things. Quickly becoming bored with conventional toys, I could be found outside playing with sticks and stones. Once I was caught cutting down the neighbor's spruce trees to build a fort.

As I grew older I strayed from my heart's desires and my imagination faded. At the age of 28, I decided to try and rediscover a simple, creative, innocent past. "Bim" (Bimbo) was the result of that search. Through the art of mime and clowning, this playful character was released, and the class clown went professional.

As "a fool and his money are soon parted," so it was my life as a performer. I supplemented my income by making willow furniture, a craft I started as a hobby in 1972. The willow furniture has grown steadily unitl, due to supply and demand, I now cannot afford to perform professionally (although I have been known to break into comic displays.)

Bent willow furniture (wicker), an early American craft, was a familiar sight on the front porches of America until the late 1930s, when modern, factory-built furniture took over. Much of the furniture was made and sold by Gypsy travelers, giving it the nickname "Gypsy twig furniture." This fits well with my Gypsy lifestyle.

My work has been in several national magazines, on T.V. and in newspapers around the country. Hopefully it will be seen soon in your home! I don't just build furniture, I build heirlooms.

Afterthought

Dwelling on the idea of writing a "How To Do It Book" I had to ask myself why? Why do I want to show people how to do the craft that I make my living at? The way I look at it, no one can do a better job of being me than me." This eliminates all the competition.

We live in a high tech world that is moving faster and faster and getting smaller and smaller. In all this chaos we look for a simpler life, one that invites nature in. Gypsy twig furniture has a rich colorful past, and by sharing my form of the craft with you, insures this art will be a part of the future. You can create something beautiful that your grand- and great-grandchildren may enjoy.

"Those who think they can and those who think they cannot are both right." Bim

This book is for those who think they can.

Willow: Family name: *SALICEAE*

This is a large group of graceful trees and shrubs that usually have slender branches and narrow leaves. There are 325 plus species of willow worldwide. About 100 species are native to North America. The smallest willow is a tiny one inch shrub that grows in Artic regions and at altitudes above the timberline. The largest willow reaches 120 ft.

In the spring willow produces upright clusters of tiny yellowish green flowers called catkins. The female flowers develop a flask-shaped pod that splits, releasing tiny seeds with white silky hairs.

Because of the pliable nature of willow it is a favorite for basket and furniture making. Willow also produces a high grade of charcoal, once used in the manufacturing of gun powder. The bark of the red willow is used for a pain reliever: aspirin. The bark also yields tannin a leather tanning substance. Willows grow near water, their interlaced roots prevent soil erosion. Willow are considered a sacred tree by many a folk tale. Here are a few species of willow that I would recommend for building:

Sand Bar Willow. A smooth bark, slender, shrub-like willow that grows in thickets. They grow close together resulting in long thin whips, great for furniture. This willow grows to be 6 inches in diameter and has a short life. It is often found in drainage areas.

Black Willow. A larger rough bark willow, this is a prime wood for furniture, but to get the whips and smaller stock you must get new growth, usually off older trees that have been cut back.

White Willow. A large 65-80 ft. tall tree. Smooth bark when young, rougher as it ages. Although it is brittle, it is good for frames.

Pussy Willow. A smooth bark, shrub-like tree, grows crooked and great for those special projects or as extra trim.

Coastal Willow. Found in the southeast U.S., this is another choice willow. Similar to black willow.

Corkscrew Willow. A hybrid created around the turn of the century, this is a valued ornamental. Its branches are twisted spirally and interwoven in the most complex way, almost as if an artist had arranged them. This is an excellent wood for adding onto furniture or to build the really unusual.

Weeping Willow. A graceful tree with long thin branches that droop down to the ground. This is the tree that most people think about when you say willow. Although it is not very suitable for furniture, it is good for baskets and small work.

The Art of Imperfection

When people start building twig furniture they attempt to make it perfect This is a difficult task when using imperfect material. There is a time when learning technique is important, but there comes a time to let the sticks teach you how beautifully imperfect Nature is.

In a world full of the man-made, factory-built, processed and packaged, many are drawn to the unusual, unique or even chaotic. A tree that grows up in a green house can be uniform on the outside, but have a shallow root system. It depends on the care and feeding of a human being. The tree that grows in the real world endures the wind, rain, draught and human encroachment, but it is a tree that has developed character. When the stick that rubbed against the fence or the burl caused by insects or the vine that has choked a tree into a spiral is placed into the right spot, it makes a difference between a piece of furniture and a work of art.

I find this principal holds as true with people, as with twigs. In learning to appreciate imperfection I am learning to except and appreciate others.

Some Basic Principles

HAVE FUN. As a child we played with sticks, they became wild horses, swords, magic wands and the list goes on, as far as our imaginations. By tapping into that child-like playfulness, a pile of sticks, a few nails, some inexpensive tools, and a little time, you can create rustic furniture. A good life is one that you can enjoy in all its simplicity."

BECOME ONE WITH THE WILLOW. Be flexible in your mind, allowing for change as the willow bends. In short, don't make it do what it doesn't want to do. Remember, that the wood begins as beautiful.

SOMETHINGNESS. In my courses I teach what I call the art of somethingness. That is the ability to see something in what others see as nothing, and creating something others will cherish. We live in a world of waste. Many things that are thrown away, with a little play/work, can become treasures. This holds true of the willows that grow along the ditches, creeks, swamps, and drainage areas. Native willow spreads quickly and with its short life span can become a nuisance, clogging drainage flow, creating a pollen problem in the spring, covering the ground with fuzzy balls (Catkins.) It is relatively easy to find people who want it removed. With somethingness you don't have to worry about art supplies for rustic furniture. Later in the book I will show you how to create something wonderful from branches of your own trees, from your own yard. Branches you might have burnt or had hauled off will become pieces of art. Things aren't always black and white when you live in a world of color."

"Bim's 3 Keys To Happiness"

1.) Establish your own high sense of order.
2.) Be constructive and creative.
3.) Don't take anything too seriously.

This vintage photograph from the turn of the century shows a willow love seat in a Victorian garden.

Harvesting the Willow

With the diameters of wood we are seeking, a set of pruning shears is the only tool that is needed. It is always best to get permission from the landowner before cutting.

Heavier stock is great for the framework This willow doesn't get more than six inches in diameter and its life span is about six years, during which it grows to 20 or 25 feet tall.

This is sandbar or swamp willow. Native to northern America, it grows in thickets or clumps, making it easy to harvest.

Lighter stock is used for bending.

This is a fine stand of willow.

This is a stand I harvested a year ago. You can see that it is coming back with a lot of suckers. This will be great for future harvesting.

An insect causes these blossoms, which I sometimes incorporate into my work.

Simple tools are all you need for rustic furniture. Start with a tape measure.

Diagonal cutter to trim off nails.

A rasp is used to clean up edges and other rough spots.

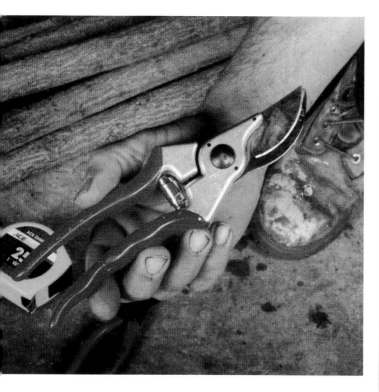

Bypass pruners allow for a close trim of branches.

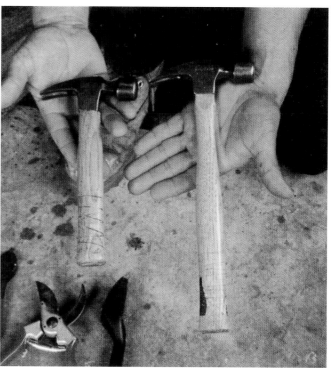

Short and long handled hammers are needed, the long handle for framing and the short for close-up work.

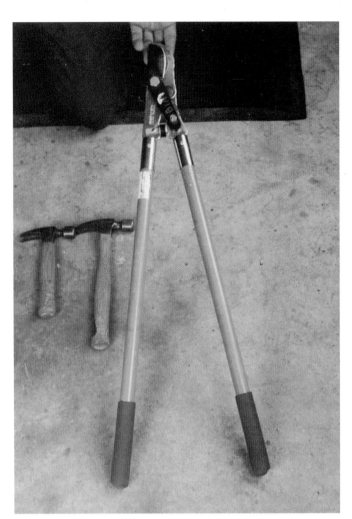

Long handled bypass loppers are a basic tool. I recommend these by Craftsman.

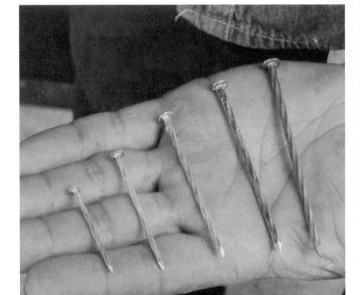

Spiral ardox gold nails in 4p, 6p, 8p, 10p and 16p sizes.

A Gypsy Twig Chair

Begin with the back legs. They are cut from stock that is 2" in diameter.

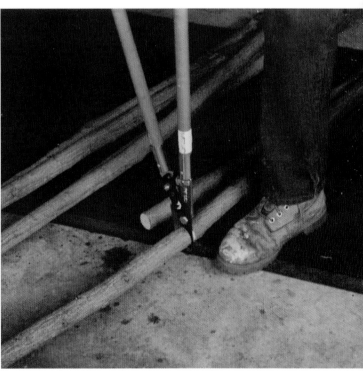

Make two legs at 33" long.

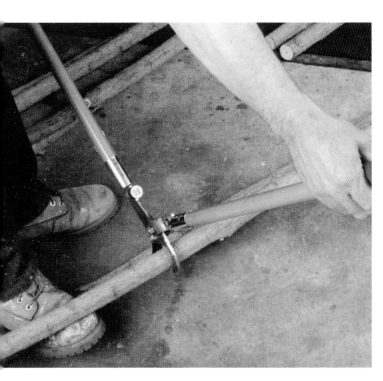

Make eight sidepieces from 1-1/2" stock. These are 27" long.

When using the lopper only the blade side should move. Support the handle of the other side against your leg so it does not move. If both sides move you tend to mar the bark because one side is dull.

Two secrets for using loppers. First, keep them sharp. Second, notice that only one edge of the lopper has an edge.

For the front legs we need two pieces that are 16" long and 2" in diameter.

Using 10p nails we can assemble the frame. Start by laying out a front and back leg. The sidepiece goes across the legs 3" from the bottom, and overhangs 1-1/2" front and back.

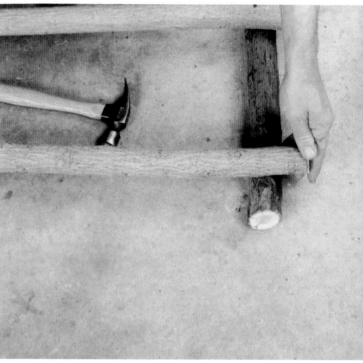

Another sidepiece crosses the front piece 10" on center above the lower one. It should overhang 1-1/2" as did the first.

Nail it in with a 10p nail, being careful not to mar the bark.

This sidepiece should slope downward as it approaches the back leg, so it crosses about 9" on center above the lower sidepiece.

When it is properly aligned, nail it in place.

and cut off the excess parallel to the leg.

Using 1-1/2" stock, make a diagonal brace between the legs. Nail in place...

Layout the other side so it mirrors the first and construct it in the same way. On this side, nail the bottom rail front and back, and nail the topside rail to the front leg only.

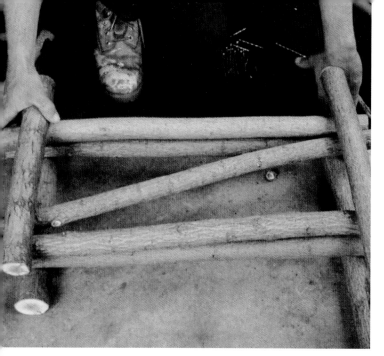

Before nailing the top side rail to the back, lay the other side on top of this one. Align the bottom of the legs...

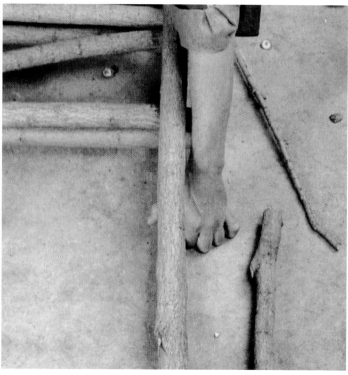

and the angle of the back leg.

the top rail...

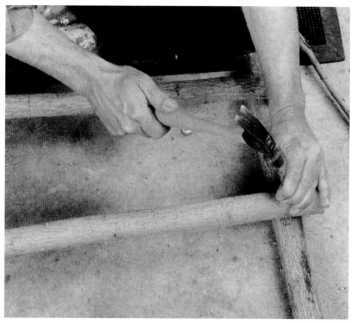

When everything aligns, nail the top side rail to the back leg.

It is important that the brace angle down toward the back leg. This distributes weight properly when you sit back in the chair, giving the structure stability.

Nail the front rail to the other side.

Pick a straight 27" piece for the front rail. With one side of the chair upright on its back, hold the front rail between your legs so it is level and nail it to the front leg above the upper side rail.

Add a bottom front rail, nailing it in place on one leg...

but checking that the front legs and the front rails are parallel before nailing the bottom rail in place.

Nail a bottom rail to the back of one leg above the brace.

Progress.

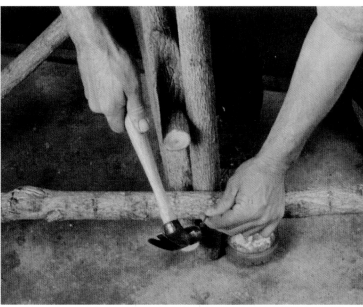

The bottom back rail will be 20" with the overlap. Using that as a guide, pull the other side of the chair into position and nail the bottom back rail.

Nail the top rail on one side.

and nail the other side.

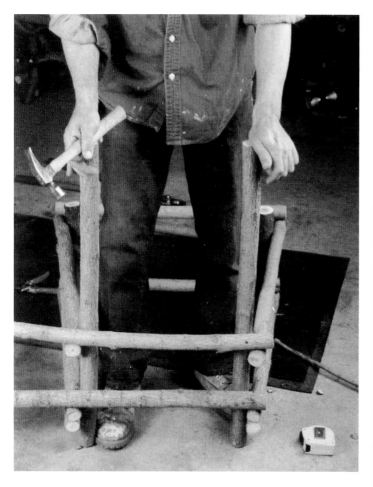

Check that the back legs are parallel...

Lop off the excess.

Progress on the basic framework.

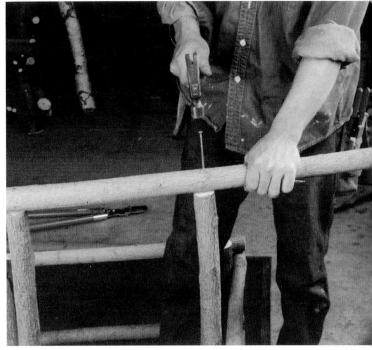

Nail both sides.

The rail at the top of the legs is 2" stock, and is nailed in place with 16p nails. Leave it long for now.

A cross piece for the seat is about 18" on center back from the front rail. Let it overhang the sides and nail in place with 10p nails.

Another cross piece goes behind the front legs. Use a piece of 1 1/2" stock that is slightly curved.

Measure a piece so it fits between the side rails about mid-way between the last two crosspieces you added.

Place behind the front legs with the curve side down, and nail into the leg from the back.

Lop it to length.

Nail in place through the side rails with 16p nails.

Nail in place with 8p nails down into the cross rails...

Using 1" diameter pieces, run a diagonal from the back seat rail to the bottom front rail inside the legs.

and sideways into the legs. The two nails give it stability against torsion.

Do the same in the back.

The arm support goes across the back 1 foot above the upper back rail. It should overhang each side by 5 or 6 inches.

Trim off the excess. One principle of working with the willow is not to nail too close to the end or cut off too close to the nail.

Make sure it is level and nail in place.

The frame is complete.

Clean up the edges before going on.

The arms are straight pieces 5 feet long and 3/4" diameter. You will need eight pieces. In the wintertime these pieces will stay pliable for a number of weeks, but in the summer they lose their elasticity in 5-7 days.

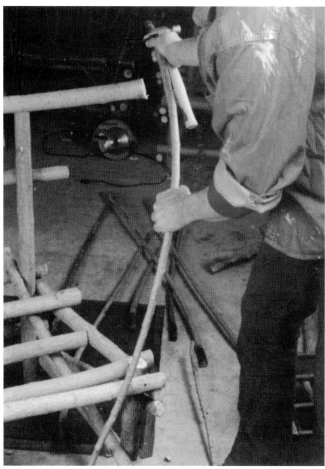

Pull the center of the piece out while bending the top back to the center back rail.

Hook the small end of the branch behind the bottom front rail inside the leg.

Nail in place at the back rail only. Use 6p nails on the small diameter pieces.

The result.

Repeat on the other side. We want to be sure the first pieces on each side are uniform and symmetrical.

Before nailing I lean the chair back to make sure the pieces are balanced.

At the top front rail the branch should cross inside the front leg about four inches in from the end.

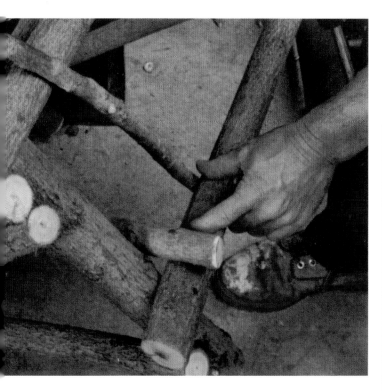

At the bottom rail there should be about 4" between the leg and the arm branch.

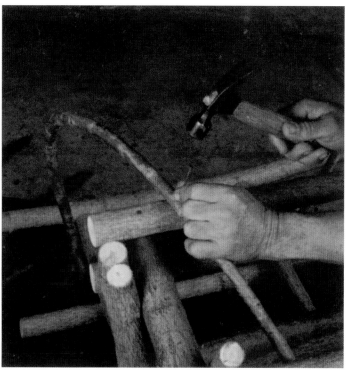

Nail in place into the top front rail.

The arms curve at the front and then flatten out toward the back.

Place the second arm piece outside the second at the bottom...

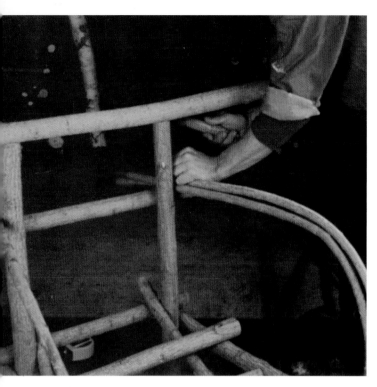

and bend it back the same way.

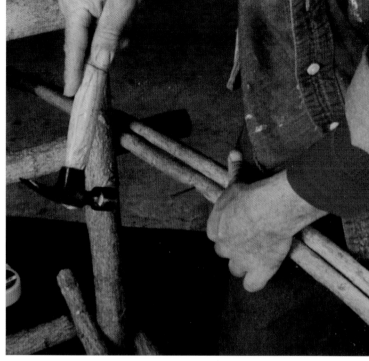

align the second arm piece with the first and drive the nail through. Your leg helps support the work at this time.

Beginning about 8 inches from the back leg, start a nail from the inside of the arm...

Continue joining the arm branches every 10-12" ...

working your way toward the bottom.

Repeat on the other side.

When you get to the top front rail, nail into it, leaving the arm branches unattached at the bottom.

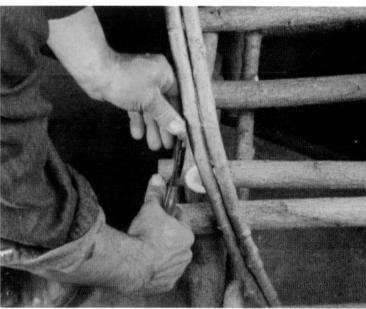

With the nail cutters, get a grip on the point of the nails, as close to the wood as you can, pull them a bit and cut them off. The pull helps set the nail.

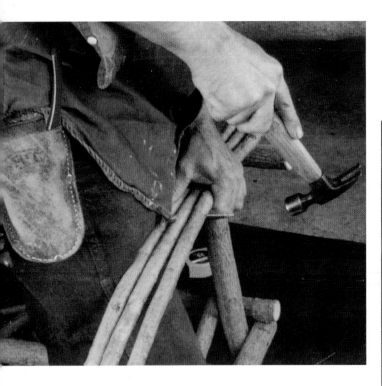

Add a third arm piece, but this time get inside the chair frame and nail from the outside.

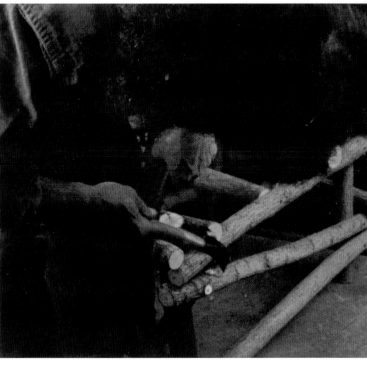

Add the fourth arm piece. It is easy to have a nail show when going from center to center. If it is on the top, be sure to remove it. It is less important underneath.

One common problem at this point is a tendency to slope the front surface of the arm back at the bend. Make sure it is nice and flat before nailing.

Lean the chair back and push the arm pieces together against the side.

Trim them off...

Nail the arm pieces in place at the bottom cross rail.

parallel to the ground.

Cut the top end of the armpieces, leaving about a 2" overhang. You may want to use loppers for this.

The arms are complete.

Prebend it and work the piece, using your foot. This helps the pliability, but also tests the piece to be certain it will not break when used in the back.

The back pieces are about 8 feet long and range from 1" to 1 1/4" in diameter.

Tuck the piece in the corner between the side rail and the inside seat brace, going just behind the back cross piece of the seat.

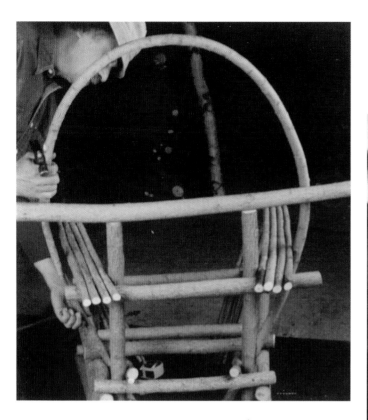

Bend it around and tuck it into the same spot on the other side.

Nail it to the top rail.

Lean the chair back and shape the loop until it is as you want it.

Cut off the ends under the chair.

Nail into the to side rail.

I'm going to trim off some excess on the arm support rail, leaving at least 1" after my last nail.

You can make the loop any shape you want, but I find that 10" from the top rail to the loop gives it a nice symmetry.

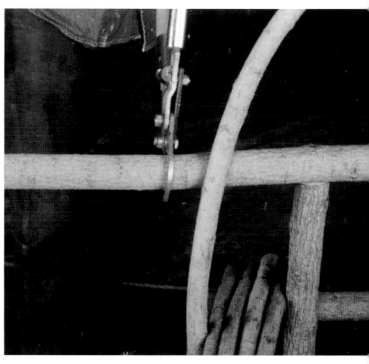

In the same way, cut the top rail.

Set a piece about 1" diameter across the front...

Nail in place with 6p nails.

trim to length, matching the other cross pieces of the seat.

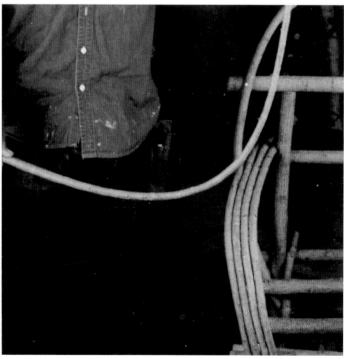

Seat pieces are about 6' long and 1/2"-3/4" in diameter at the thick end. Prebend the piece.

Align it in the center of the seat...

and here using 4p nails.

and nail in place here...\

Before nailing at the top, make sure the back has a nice curve to it.

Working out from the center slat, the next pieces should be about 1" from the first in the seat...

Continue to add the other slats in the same way.

flaring out to 2" at the top rail. Be sure the surface created by the two slats is flat.

Trim off any branch knobs as you go.

I trim the tops to get them out of my way. Leave about 4 -5 inches.

After it is cut the slat falls right into place.

To trim the bottom ends I place my cutter just behind the cross piece.

Nail the bottom end in place with 4p nails.

Returning to the back, prebend another back piece.

Bend it around, going in front of the slats...

The branches are naturally thinner at one end than the other. I started here with the narrow end, so this time I'll start with the thick. Succeeding pieces will alternate thick and thin, creating a balanced result.

and tuck it into the other side.

Align the second bow with first

The nail should go all the way through. Clinch the nail on the other side by hammering it over.

and nail them together with a 6p nail.

Working around, put an 8p nail into the frame.

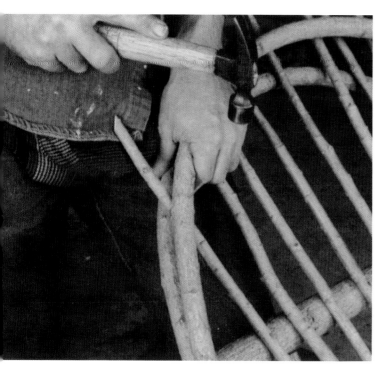

Spread the slats a little and nail through them to the back bow using 6p nails.

When you have finished, trim off the ends of the bow.

Continue across the slats. With this double bow method, the chair withstands the test of time.

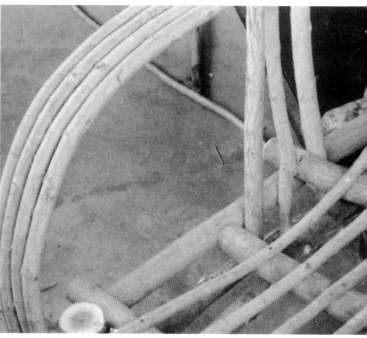

It is difficult to get the multiple bows to create a flat surface. I begin by inserting it in front of the previous bow into the base of the chair.

I then hold the end of the twig under my armpit, pulling it back behind the chair.

I can then bring the bow forward, forcing the line into a flat surface.

I then nail the two bows together just below the top rail where they meet.

One nail to hold it in position...

Then I tuck the free end into the other side.

Pull the nails through to set them, then cut off the ends.

Go back and nail the bows together, using 6p nails.

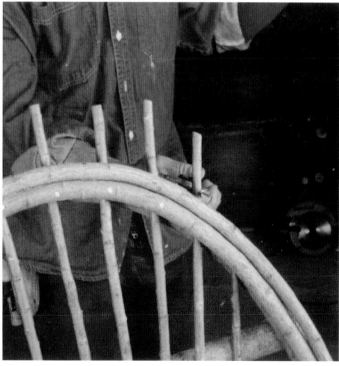

Trim off the spindles a couple inches from where you nailed them.

Follow the same method for the last two bows.

The final piece is a curved brace for the front. With the chair on its back nail at one side into the bottom cross piece...

The back complete.

the center...

Trim off the excess.

and the other side.

Finished

Project 2: An Endtable

The tabletop is rough sawn bass wood, about 18" x 16" x 5/4". To smooth it up a little, I use a rasp.

In all four corners I place a 10p nail 2" in from each side...

and drive it all the way through.

We use four 24" legs, 1 1/2" - 2" in diameter.

43

Push one leg onto each nail.

Using your legs as a support, nail a crosspiece about six inches from the bottom on two of the legs. Nail one side...

Turn the legs so that if there is any curve in them it is outward.

Check to be sure that the legs splay out, then nail the other side.

Do the same on the opposite side.

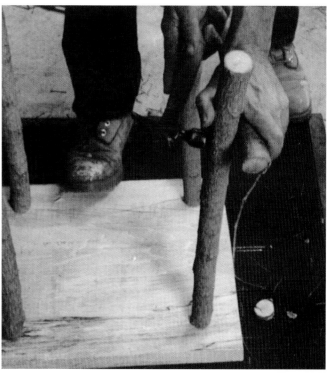

If the nails come through, either clinch them or cut them off. In this area I usually clinch them for better strength.

Before nailing the second nail, check the alignment with the other end.

Add the other cross pieces. After the first nail...

stop to check the spread and continue with the second.

Cut off the excess.

Do the same on the other side, making sure everything is square.

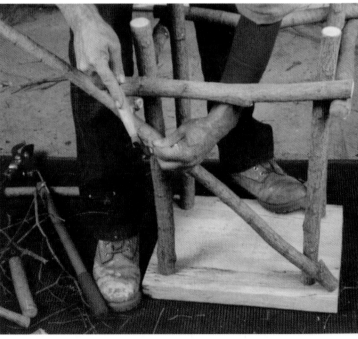

When everything is square add diagonal braces, nailing them with 8p nails into the legs...

at each end.

When the four braces are on, cut off the excess.

Continue all the way around. At each step, be sure that things are still squared and haven't become twisted.

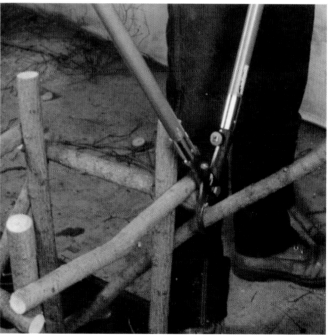

The best way of cutting diagonals with the loppers is from the top.

If all the legs are the same length and I got things straight, it should be level when I turn it over. In this case it is just little wobbly. Looking carefully I determine that one leg is just a bit long.

It is only a slight wobble, so I take off only 1/8".

Looking down I can see that this leg is the culprit.

I want to add an edge. Using a branch the same diameter as the thickness of the tabletop, I nail it first in the center.

Nail one end, being careful not to go too close to it.

Repeat at the opposite end.

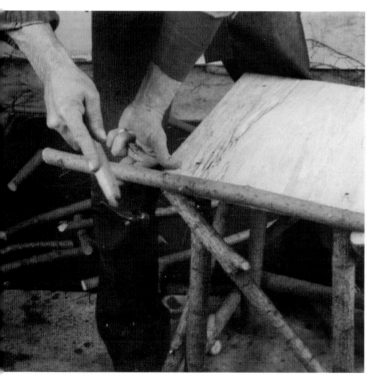

Then nail the other.

Trim the ends of the trim flush with the sides, by laying the lopper blade against the edge of the tabletop.

Then add the trim to the side, overlapping the end piece.

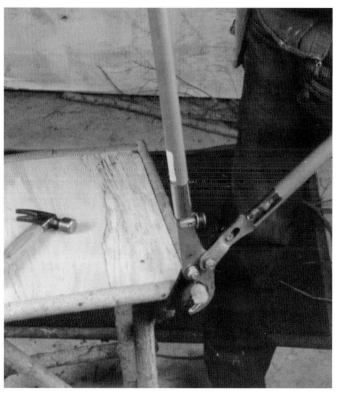

Add the final trim piece and cut to fit.

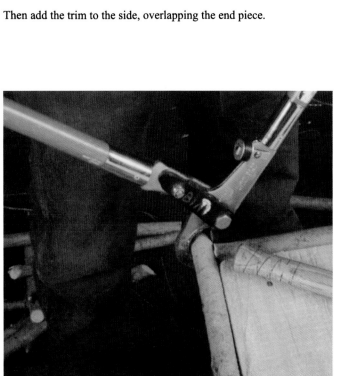

When trimming the ends, lay the blade along side of the trim and cut from above.

Clean up the edges with the rasp.

The basic table.

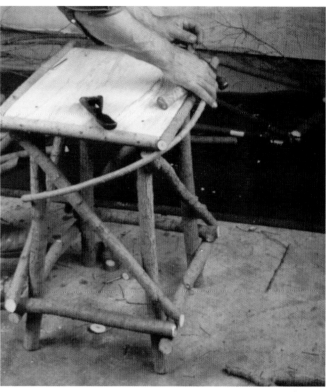

I can bend it around...

You can add details to the table in a variety of ways. I use some 1/2"
branches to add decorative flourishes. Nailing it here at the bottom...

up over the corner of the top, where I nail it again.

Then I take it back under the table nailing it to the leg and weaving the fine ends through the bottom.

Do the same thing from the opposite corner with a second branch.

When the curves are established, you can nail it at the various intersections.

Project 3: Birdfeeder

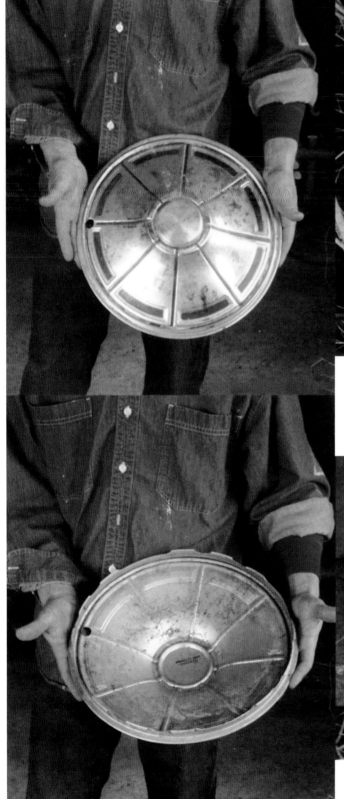

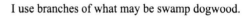

I use branches of what may be swamp dogwood.

I want to make a tripod of the branches. I cross two branches at the crotch...

One of my favorite things is to take found objects and make something unique out of them. I found this hubcap in a willow patch (you find lots of things in willow patches). It should make a great birdfeeder. This is fun because you can't really screw it up.

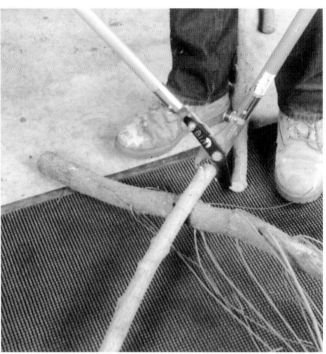

Trim off the end of the brace.

and nail them together. The size of the nail depends on what you're nailing through and what you're nailing into.

At the bottom of the X formed by the two branches, add a cross-piece, 1" - 1 1/2" in diameter. The size is not as important as the strength it gives to the piece.

Stand it up and add the third leg, through the crotch.

Nail the branches together at the crotch.

This will take at least two nails.

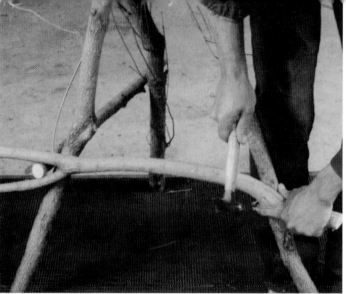

Add crosspieces around the base.

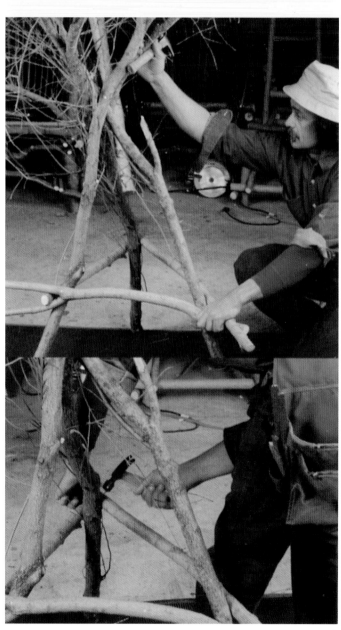

Before the final nail, check on how the piece sets and looks. Make adjustments as necessary.

Prune off the excess wood at the braces.

Unfortunately, the hubcap is not quite level.

Set the hubcap roughly in place and remove any branches in the way.

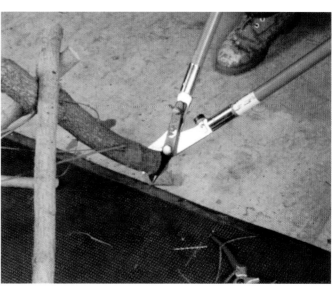

I take care of that by cutting a little off of one leg.

Continue to trim until the hubcap sits securely in place. I have managed to get a small branch to go through the air stem hole.

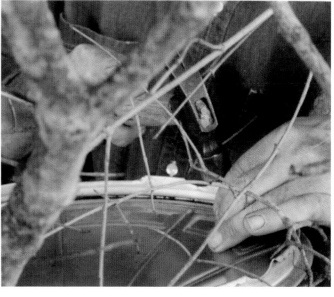

Nail the hubcap in place.

Nail some of the branches together. This not only gives added stability, it adds to the shape.

This is also a good time to prune off any unsightly spots, like this broken limb.

A branch that comes out at an odd angle like this...

can be bent and nailed to another.

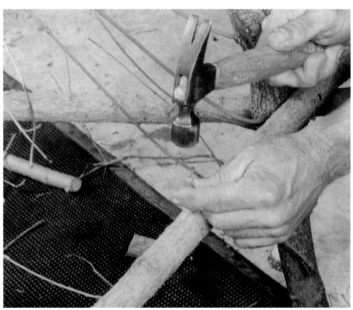

When I am pleased with the top, I can add some of the prunings around the base. To blind nail a piece to the brace, I drive a nail half way into it ...

and cut the end off at an angle.

This gives me a sharp point.

I can push another branch on to the nail. If the wood is too hard I may have to resort to nailing from beneath.

Nail the added branch securely to the others.

The result.

59

Gallery

Finishing

If you had fun and did your best at that time, your piece is perfect. No one can do a better job at being you. Don't judge yourself by your past or your future, only your now. Have fun, give it your best shot and you can't screw it up. This gives you a confidence to finish and a passion to create more.